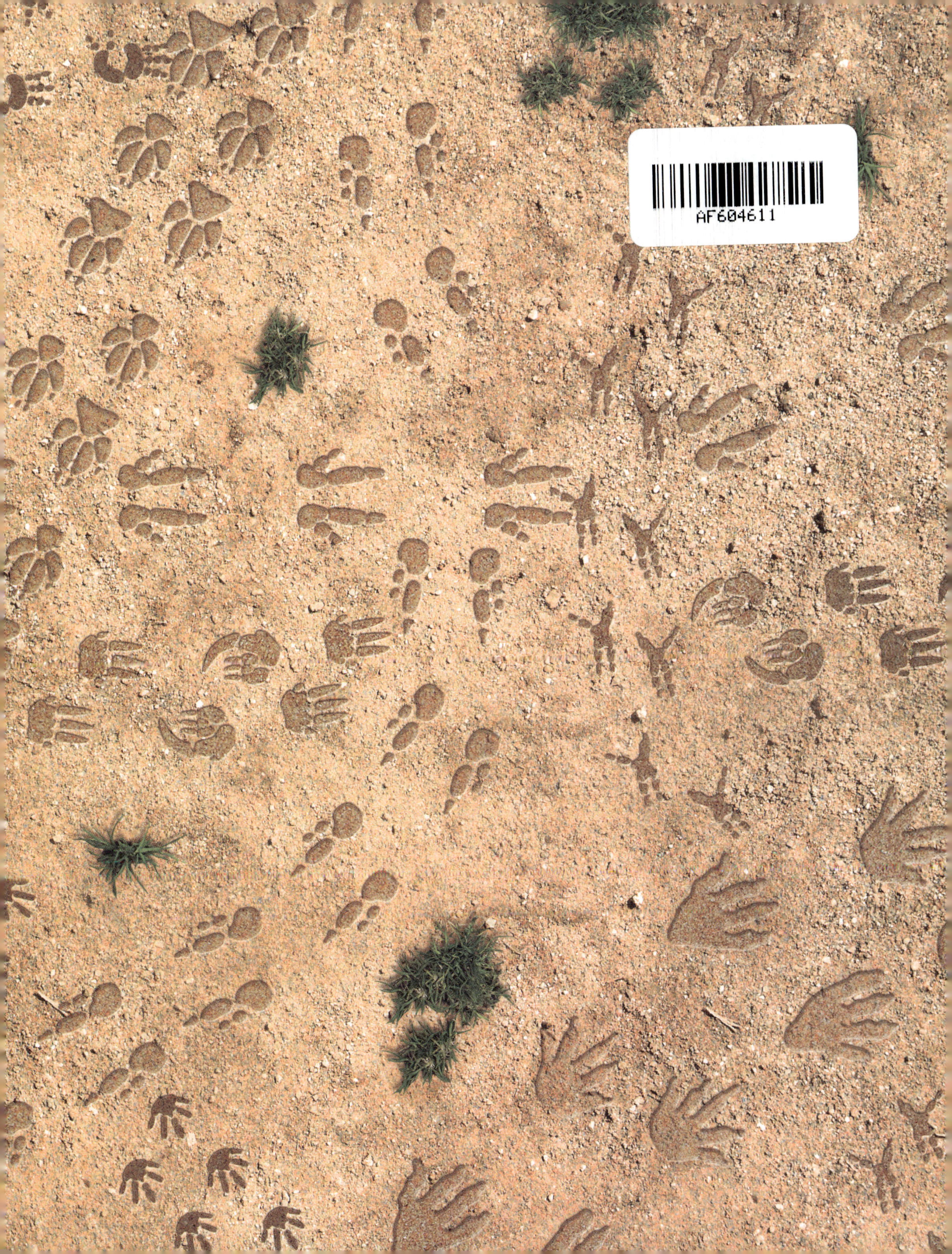

JOHN LESLEY

AUSTRALIA'S REMARKABLE WILDLIFE

EMU

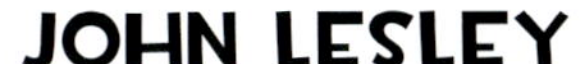

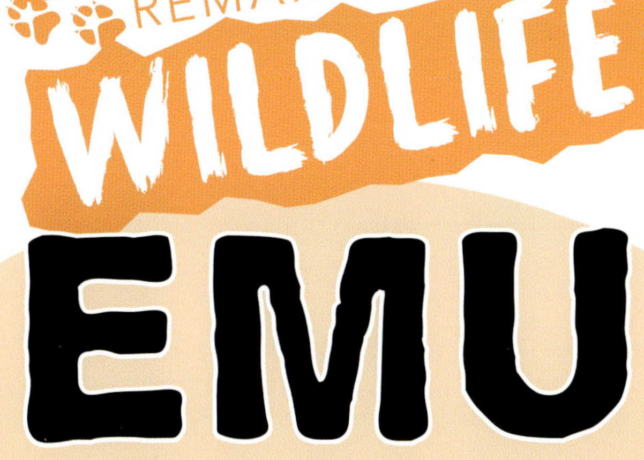

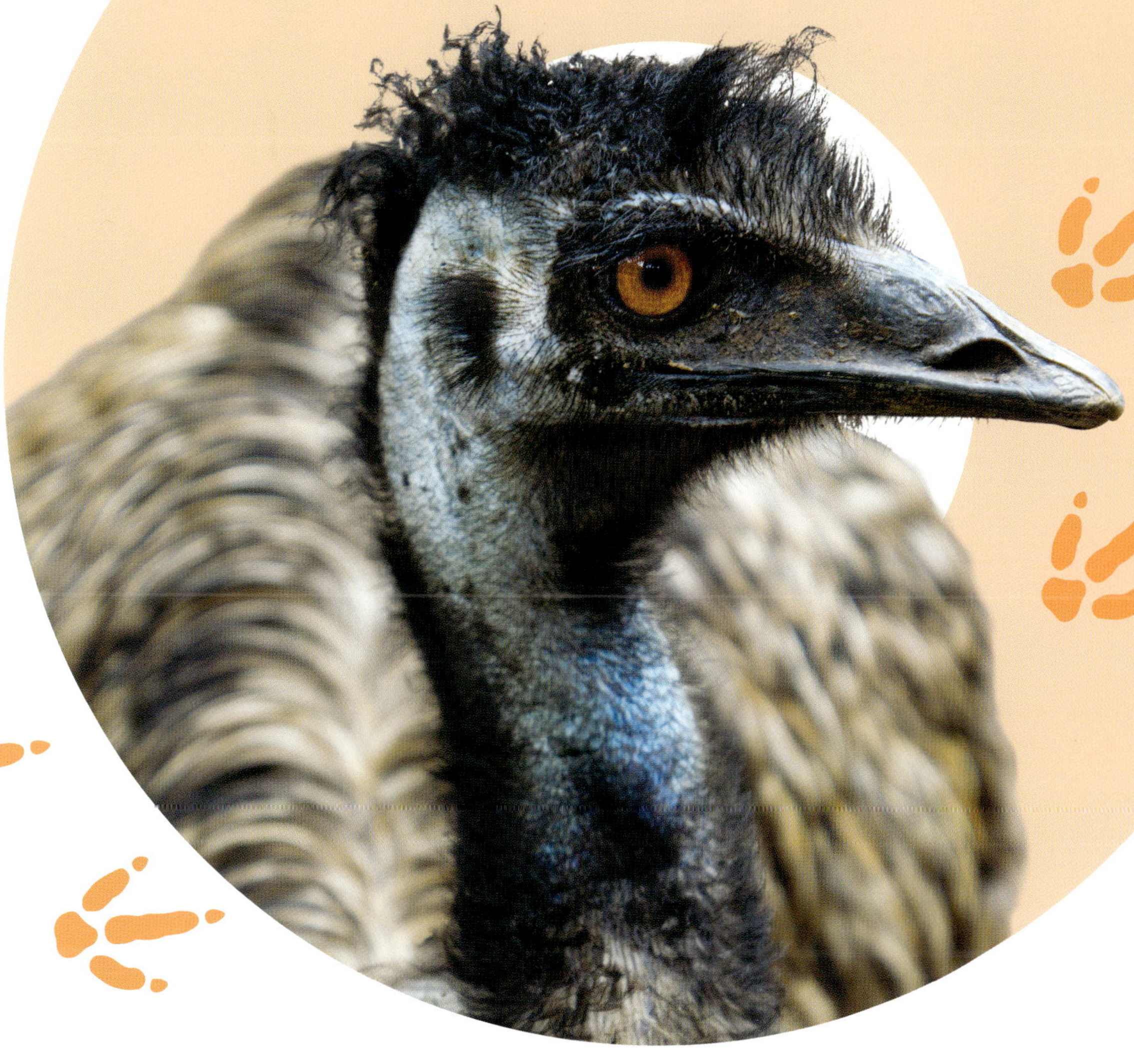

REDBACK publishing

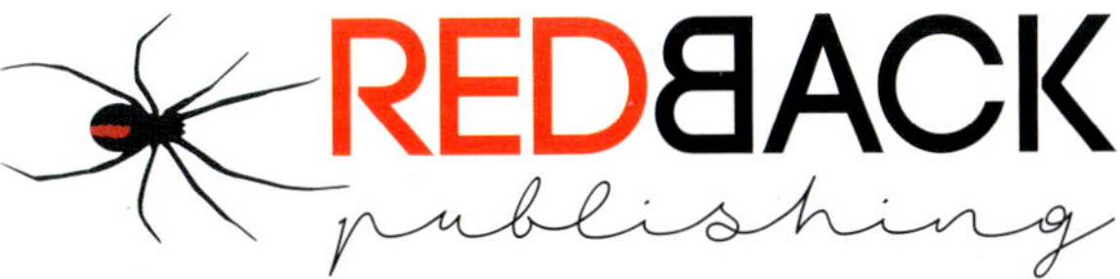

First Published 2024 by
Redback Publishing
Suite 6, 13a Narabang Way,
Belrose NSW 2085
Australia

www.redbackpublishing.com
info@redbackpublishing.com

ISBN 978-1-761400-69-8

Author: John Lesley
Editor: Caroline Thomas
Design: Redback Publishing

A catalogue record for this book is available from the National Library of Australia

Original illustrations © Redback Publishing 2024
Originated by Redback Publishing

Acknowledgements
Abbreviations: l—left, r—right,
b—bottom, t—top, c—centre, m—middle
We would like to thank the following for permission to reproduce photographs: (Images © shutterstock)
p6bl Judi Lapsley Miller, CC BY 4.0 <https://creativecommons.org/licenses/by/4.0>, via Wikimedia Commons, p13bl Joshua Tagicakibau, CC BY-SA 4.0 <https://creativecommons.org/licenses/by-sa/4.0>, via Wikimedia Commons, p18bc William Porden Kay, Public domain, via Wikimedia Commons, p19tl ARC CoE CABAH, CC BY-SA 4.0 <https://creativecommons.org/licenses/by-sa/4.0>, via Wikimedia Commons, p25cr Auckland Museum, CC BY 4.0 <https://creativecommons.org/licenses/by/4.0>, via Wikimedia Commons

CONTENTS

WHAT IS AN EMU?

The emu has a long neck, long legs, and a large body. It is one of the iconic animals of the Australian Outback. Generally thought to be not very intelligent, the emu nevertheless survives and multiplies in some of the driest and hottest habitats in the country.

The emu is a bird that cannot fly. It is the tallest bird in Australia, but the ostrich from Africa is the biggest bird in the world. It is taller and heavier than the emu.

Ostrich

Along with the kangaroo, the emu is a symbol of Australia. Both animals hold up the shield on the Australian Coat of Arms, so the image of an emu is present on government buildings and in official documents throughout the Nation.

4K UHD
REC
00:35:02
4K UHD
00:35:02

RATITES

The emu is in a group of birds called ratites. This group also includes the ostrich from Africa, the cassowary that lives in Queensland rainforests, the rhea from South America, and even the little kiwi from New Zealand.

All ratites are flightless and have lost the special types of feathers needed for flight. Ratite feathers are long, thin and useless for flying.

Rhea

Cassowary

Ostrich

Little spotted kiwi

ADAPTATIONS

Being able to fly requires a lot of energy and special body adaptations, such as flight muscles, feathers, and light, hollow bones.

Ratites do not need to spend so much energy on flight, and instead they have evolved other ways of feeding and escaping predators.

Emus and other ratites do not have the special breastbone that enables flight. This is the bone that is attached to the strong flight muscles in other birds.

With the exception of the little kiwi, ratites have long legs, are good runners, and they protect themselves with their vicious claws.

EMU BASIC FACTS

SCIENTIFIC NAME

The emu's scientific name is *Dromaius novaehollandiae*, which translated refers to a running creature from New Holland, the old European name for Australia.

The common name, emu, probably comes from a Portuguese word, used when European sailors first landed on the western coast of Australia and saw the bird and its tracks.

SIZE & SHAPE

At nearly two metres high, and weighing up to 55 kilograms, the adult emu is a formidable sight. Most of the height is due to its long neck and long legs. The thin feathers provide insulation against heat and cold. They may also be dense enough to deter a predator such as a dingo from biting into the body.

SOUNDS

An emu can make loud drumming and grunting noises in its throat to communicate with other birds. The father emu whistles to his offspring to stop them wandering too far away.

COLOUR

Feathers: grey

Eye: bright orange

Upper neck: bare, bluish skin

Head: black, hair-like band of feathers runs from the beak back across the head, and down to the back of the neck

CONSERVATION STATUS

The emu is not presently under any threat of extinction. Living in open forests and semi-arid areas, where the human population is low, helps to keep the emu safe from loss of habitat. The great care taken with raising the young until they are old enough to defend themselves also contributes to emu numbers remaining stable.

THE EMU BODY

ADAPTATIONS

Having lost its ability to fly, the emu has a number of adaptations that replace the advantages that flying gives other birds.

PROTECTION

Emus protect themselves by having sharp eyesight, a long neck so they can see what is in the distance, and strong legs and claws that they use to kick and strike an enemy.

EYES

Living in the dust of an arid region means that grit can get into the eyes. The emu has an extra, clear eyelid that is used to protect and wipe over its eyes.

KEEPING STEADY

Since it can run so fast, the emu needs to be able to keep a steady eye on what is around it. Watch an emu's head as it runs and you will see that the head does not bob up and down at all. The eyes are kept at a steady level, so the emu knows exactly what is around it and where it is going.

WINGS

The little wings may be useless for flight, but the emu spreads them out when running to help balance itself. Spreading the wings also helps the emu cool down.

RUNNING

Some emus can reach the amazing speed of nearly 50 kph. Running at 20 kph, which is a top speed for a human athlete, is easy for an emu. The feet have only three toes and they all point forward, making fast running possible.

EMU IN THE SKY

ORIGINS

Australian Indigenous people saw an image of the emu when they studied the stars and constellations of the night sky over Australia. The Emu in the Sky spans much of the Milky Way galaxy.

PATTERNS

European astronomers looked at the patterns that stars made in the sky, and gave the constellations names, such as Orion, the Southern Cross and Scorpius.

Acrux is the star at the bottom of the Southern Cross.

Australian Indigenous rock art, Northern Territory, Australia

STARS AND SHAPES

Australian Indigenous astronomers look at both the stars and the dark spaces between them. One of the shapes they see is that of an emu. When this shape moves across the sky as the seasons pass, the position of the Emu in the Sky is an important way of determining when certain tasks need to be done, and when various food sources are available.

EMU HABITATS

Emus are native to Australia and do not live in the wild in any other country. Since they have evolved to run fast, they do not like to be in dense bushland or in rainforests. They prefer to live in open plains in semi-arid areas, and in open forests mixed with grassland.

Emus depend on being able to raise their head up high to see predators in the distance, which is another reason why they prefer open areas. The young emus stay together in a mob for protection, so dense bushland would not be a safe habitat since a predator would be able to separate one bird and attack it more easily.

Emus live in every State and Territory except for Tasmania. Farmers often find them feeding in paddocks. Emus will travel long distances in search of food and climate conditions that are the most suitable for raising their young.

The Snowy Mountains region of New South Wales is also a habitat for emus, which can survive in the snow for short periods. In very cold conditions, they are likely to move to areas where the weather is not so harsh.

EMU LIFE CYCLE

LIFESPAN

In the wild, emus can live for over ten years. Farmed emus are killed when they are about two years old.

MATING

Depending on the time of year, adult emus can be either solitary, or seen with their mate or chicks, or in a mob with other emus. When the cooler months and the dry season comes, emus find a mate, prepare a flat nest on the ground, and stay together until the female lays her large eggs.

FAMILY GROUPS

The group of young emus will stay together for a long time, before they finally mature and leave to live by themselves before they find a mate. If you see a mob of emus together, it is likely they are all from the same clutch of eggs.

EGGS

Emus are birds and they lay eggs, just like other birds do. The difference with the emu is that the egg is very large at 13 centimetres long, dark green and thick-shelled.

THE MALE EMU

After laying her eggs, the female leaves the male to raise the chicks by himself. He stays with them for many months after they hatch, making sure they are ready to look after themselves before he goes off to lead his solitary life again. The chicks are striped with light and dark grey colouring, an adaptation that helps to hide them from predators.

EMU ANCESTORS

GONDWANA BREAKS UP

Emus may have ancient ancestors that lived on the continent called Gondwana, which existed millions of years ago. Gondwana has since broken up into separate landmasses including Africa, Australia and South America.

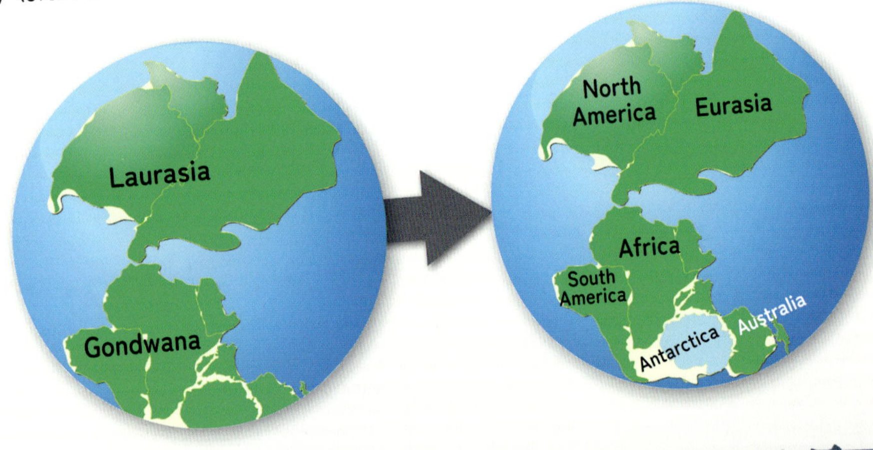

There used to be small emus present in Australia, but these have become extinct since European colonisation began in 1788.

This watercolour by William Porden Kay depicts emus at Stanley, Tasmania during the 1840s.

Genyornis newtoni is an extinct species of large, flightless bird that lived in Australia until around 50,000 years ago.

THUNDER BIRDS AND MOA

Although emus look like smaller versions of the terrifyingly huge thunder birds of ancient Australia, or the moa of ancient New Zealand, they are not closely related to either of them.

The moa statue at Bealey, New Zealand, welcomes visitors to the West Coast of the South Island.

Being flightless is a feature that has evolved separately in different types of birds, but that usually results in them having similar features such as long legs and necks.

EMU FOOD

Emus are omnivores, although their main diet consists of grasses, leaves, fruit, seeds and many other edible plants.

Emus will also eat insects, lizards, mice, snails and other small wildlife. Birds that are normally herbivores will often change their diet when they are producing eggs. The extra protein they need at that time will sometimes cause them to seek out insects or small animals to eat as well as their normal plant diet.

Emus enclosed on farms need a special ratite feed that is sold by various specialist suppliers. They cannot survive on the sort of food that farmers feed to poultry, since their bone structure and weight require different nutrients for the emu to be healthy.

Living in the semi-arid regions of Australia means that emus need to be able to locate water.

They can smell water from kilometres away. Emus can swim and their thick feathers are very good at holding a large amount of water. This helps to keep them cool under the hot sun but adds kilos to the weight they have to carry around.

THREATS TO THE EMU

IUCN RED LIST

The Red List is an international list of living things and their conservation status. According to the Red List, the emu is not currently under any threat of extinction.

HUMANS

As with nearly all wildlife on Earth, the main threats to the emu come from humans and our activities. Illegal hunting and the destruction of natural habitats pose the main threat to the continued survival of emus.

PREDATORS

A large, fully grown and healthy emu is easily able to protect itself from the feral dogs and dingoes that might try to attack it. Chicks, and small or sick emus are very much under threat from attack by predators. Eagles, pythons and large lizards will attack and eat emu chicks.

PROTECTING THEMSELVES

The emu's strong legs and sharp claws are weapons that it uses against anything that threatens it. Even a harmless creature that comes too close and frightens the emu can expect to be stomped on, kicked and possibly killed.

Emus are known for killing snakes that slither near them. On emu farms, dogs and cats need to be kept well away or they could become victims too.

EMUS AND PEOPLE

ROADS

Emus are a great danger on roads, both to themselves and to drivers. They run back and forth in zigzags, which is their way of confusing a predator. Unfortunately, this habit also makes them more liable to be hit by a car or truck on a road. Hitting a big, heavy emu will kill or injure the bird, but can also cause the human driver to crash.

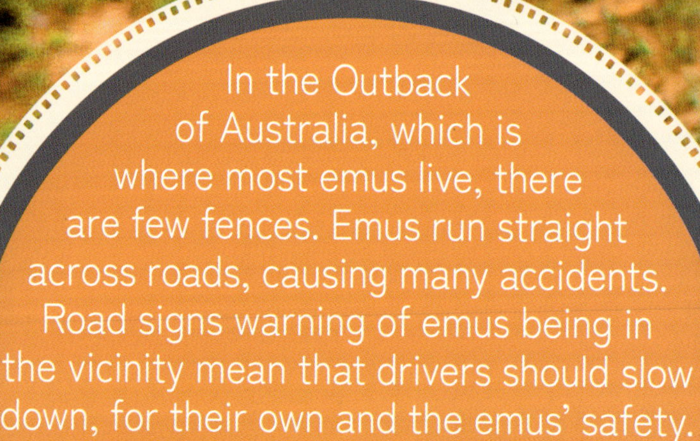

In the Outback of Australia, which is where most emus live, there are few fences. Emus run straight across roads, causing many accidents. Road signs warning of emus being in the vicinity mean that drivers should slow down, for their own and the emus' safety.

EMU FARMS

Emus are farmed for their meat, feathers and skin. Oil from emus used to be considered a medicine for just about every illness. Emu feathers are not as magnificent as those of the ostrich, but they are used to add to hats and for other craft work. The soft leather is made into bags and belts.

EMU ARTWORK

In the past, the big, green emu eggs were collected and emptied to make ornaments for Victorian-era homes. The thick shell made a firm base for artistic carving, and a carved emu egg became a fashionable addition to the household decorations. Artists working with emu eggs today need a special licence from the government.

Despite all this use for farming, it is illegal to collect eggs or animals from the wild. All emus used for farming purpose must be bred from animals that are already on farms or captive.

WHERE TO SEE AN EMU

THE OUTBACK

Emus travel long distance across their Outback habitats. They are often seen in mobs running across grasslands.

ZOOS

Zoos are the best place to get up close to an emu and see what it looks like in detail. Never get too close though, as they peck and kick without warning. They are also very attracted to anything shiny and will try to take jewellery.

EMU FARMS

A few emu farms sometimes allow visits from members of the public.

SORTING ANIMALS INTO GROUPS

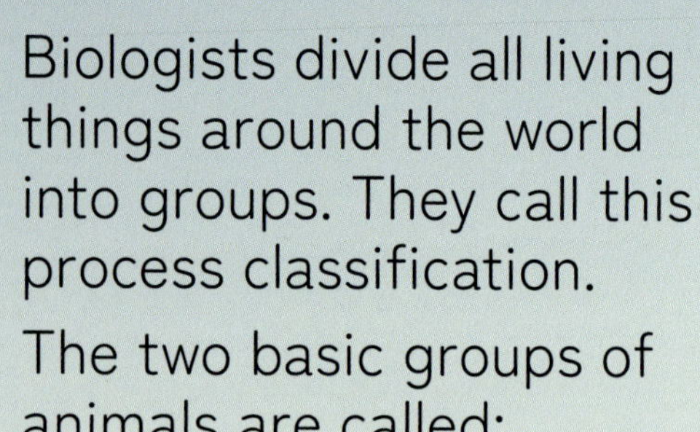

Biologists divide all living things around the world into groups. They call this process classification.

The two basic groups of animals are called:

VERTEBRATES

Vertebrates have a backbone

INVERTEBRATES

Invertebrates do not have a backbone

Vertebrates are further divided into these groups (classes). Emus are birds and belong in the class called Aves.

EMUS AND OSTRICHES

Emus and ostriches are the two tallest ratite birds in the world. Neither can fly.

Find out below how they are alike and how they differ.

HOW THEY DIFFER

ADULT EMU	ADULT OSTRICH
Runs at up to 50 kph	Runs at up to 70 kph
Up to 2 m high	Just under 3 m high
Weighs about 55 kg	Weighs about 150 kg
Long, thin feathers	Large feathers used for display when mating
Native of Australia	Native of Africa
Chicks are striped	Chicks are spotted grey
Runs on 3 toes on each foot	Runs on 2 toes on each foot

Ostrich family

Emus and ostriches are omnivores

HOW THEY ARE THE SAME

- Male raises the chicks
- Omnivores
- Flightless
- Long legs and neck
- Very large eggs

Emus and ostriches are flightless

Ostrich hatching

Emu eggs

GLOSSARY

adaptation change in a living thing to make it better able to survive

breastbone bone in middle of chest

clutch group of eggs in a nest

dense very thick

formidable strong and scary

hollow being empty inside

mob group of emus

semi-arid having a low rainfall

solitary being alone

stable remaining the same

zigzag having a back-and-forth shape or movement

INDEX